TOOLS FOR CAREGIVERS

- **F&P LEVEL:** C
- **WORD COUNT:** 32
- **CURRICULUM CONNECTIONS:** machines

Skills to Teach

- **HIGH-FREQUENCY WORDS:** a, big, has, in, is, it, on, the
- **CONTENT WORDS:** chute, concrete, down, drives, drum, goes, mixes, out, play, pours, sets, truck, turns, we
- **PUNCTUATION:** exclamation point, periods
- **WORD STUDY:** /k/, spelled c (concrete); /k/, spelled ck (truck); long /a/, spelled ay (play); /ow/, spelled ou (out); /ow/, spelled ow (down); /sh/, spelled ch (chute)
- **TEXT TYPE:** information report

Before Reading Activities

- Read the title and give a simple statement of the main idea.
- Have students "walk" through the book and talk about what they see in the pictures.
- Introduce new vocabulary by having students predict the first letter and locate the word in the text.
- Discuss any unfamiliar concepts that are in the text.

After Reading Activities

One of the book's content words, "concrete," uses the letter /c/ as a hard /k/ sound. Give readers more examples, such as "cat" and "car." What other words can readers name that use /c/ as a hard /k/ sound? Write their answers on the board.

Tadpole Books are published by Jump!, 5357 Penn Avenue South, Minneapolis, MN 55419, www.jumplibrary.com
Copyright ©2025 Jump. International copyright reserved in all countries. No part of this book may be reproduced in any form without written permission from the publisher.
Editor: Jenna Gleisner **Designer:** Emma Almgren-Bersie
Photo Credits: Another77/Shutterstock, cover; kozmoat98/iStock, 1; RiverNorthPhotography/iStock, 2tl, 8–9; RichLegg/iStock, 2tr, 14–15; Benjamin Crone/Alamy, 2ml, 4–5; Alekswolff/Dreamstime, 2mr, 6–7; ungvar/Shutterstock, 2bl, 10–11; Carolyn Franks/Shutterstock, 2br, 12–13; Art Konovalov/Shutterstock, 3; LHBLLC/Shutterstock, 16.
Library of Congress Cataloging-in-Publication Data
Names: Gleisner, Jenna Lee, author.
Title: Mixers / by Jenna Lee Gleisner.
Description: Minneapolis, MN: Jump!, Inc., [2025]
Series: Machines on the move | Includes index.
Audience: Ages 3–6
Identifiers: LCCN 2024021379 (print)
LCCN 2024021380 (ebook)
ISBN 9798892135986 (hardcover)
ISBN 9798892135993 (paperback)
ISBN 9798892136006 (ebook)
Subjects: LCSH: Concrete mixers—Juvenile literature. | Readers (Primary)
Classification: LCC TA439 .G545 2025 (print)
LCC TA439 (ebook)
DDC 629.225—dc23/eng/20240508
LC record available at https://lccn.loc.gov/2024021379
LC ebook record available at https://lccn.loc.gov/2024021380

MACHINES ON THE MOVE
MIXERS

by Jenna Lee Gleisner

TABLE OF CONTENTS

Words to Know	2
Mix It	3
Let's Review!	16
Index	16

WORDS TO KNOW

chute

concrete

drum

mixes

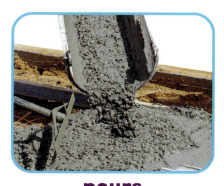
pours

sets

MIX IT

A truck drives.

drum

It has a big drum.

It turns.

concrete

Concrete is in it.

It mixes.

It goes down the chute.

It pours out.

It sets.

We play on it!

LET'S REVIEW!

Concrete mixers are big machines! What part of the machine is this?

INDEX

chute 9
concrete 6
drives 3

drum 4
mixes 7
pours 11